JavaServer Faces

Interview Questions

You'll Most Likely Be Asked

Job Interview Questions Series

www.vibrantpublishers.com

JavaServer Faces Interview Questions
You'll Most Likely Be Asked

ISBN-10: 1461016681
ISBN-13: 978-14-61016-68-7

Library of Congress Control Number: 2011925571

The publisher wishes to thank Alexandru Popoiu (Romania) for his invaluable inputs to this edition.

Contents

This page is intentionally left blank

JavaServer Faces Questions

Review these typical interview questions and think about how you would answer them. Read the answers listed; you will find best possible answers along with strategies and suggestions.

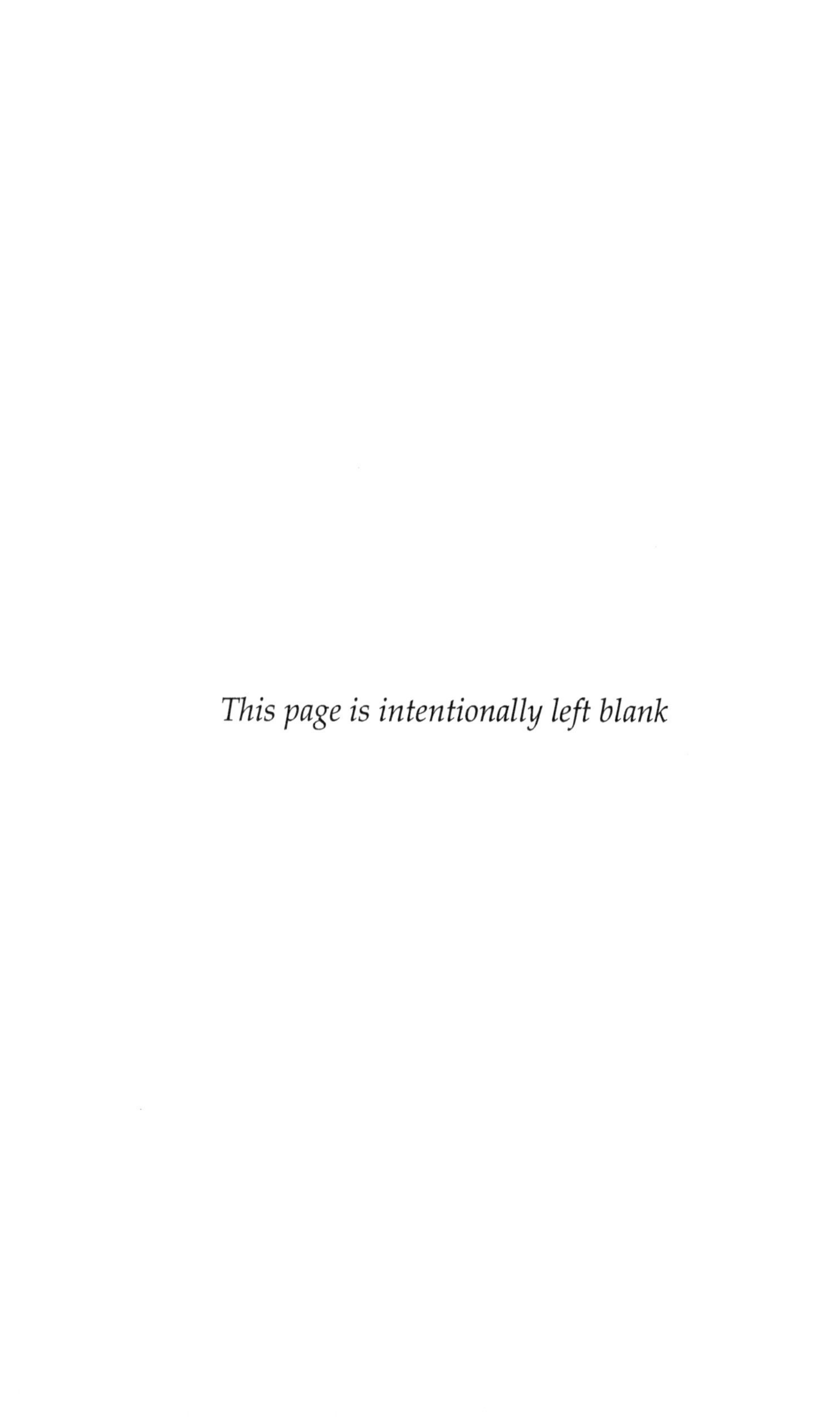
This page is intentionally left blank

Introduction to JSF

1: What is JSF and what does it do?

Answer:

JSF stands for *JavaServer Faces* and it is a component based framework used for the development of user interface of web applications.

2: What components can we find in JSF?

Answer:

JSF comprises of three parts, they are:

a) The prefabricated UI,
b) The event driven programming model and
c) A component model which ensures that third party developers are able to supply additional components.

3: How many versions of JSF are currently on the market and which are these?

Answer:

At the moment JSF has three versions: the first one is the 1.0, second is the upgraded 1.2 version and the newer, improved version is 2.0. This version is much easier to use and provides new features such as AJAX integration.

4: What is the advantage of using JSF?

Answer:

JSF is mainly used because it is a standard that incorporates multiple implementations. It has been designed from the ground up by a standards committee that ensures the product is constantly improved and updated.

5: How can JSF be used for designing web applications?

Answer:

JSF is used by both designers and programmers alike by separating and containing the application code in *Beans* and the design in web pages.

6: What are *Beans* in JSF?

Answer:

A *Bean* is a class that exposes properties and also events to a framework, with the property being a named value of a given type that can be either read or written.

7: What is a Managed *Bean* in JSF?

Answer:

A *Managed Bean* is also a Java *Bean*, but it can be accessed from a JSF page. It must also have a name and a scope, making the *Bean* available for one user across multiple pages. More bluntly put, *Managed Beans* are conduits between the user interface and the back end of the application.

8: What are JSF pages?

Answer:

A *JSF page* is similar to an HTML *Form;* each browser screen needs one. There are some differences though: the page must be properly formatted XHTML and instead of head, body and *Form* the *h:head, h:body* and *h:form* tags are used.

9: What services does JSF offer?

Answer:

JSF offers a total seven services, they are:

a) Model View Controller Architecture,
b) Data Conversion,
c) Validation and Error handling,
d) Custom components,
e) Internationalization,
f) Alternative Renderers and
g) AJAX support.

10: Which are the six distinct phases defined by a JSF specification?

Answer:

The six phases are:

a) Restore view,
b) Apply request values,
c) Process validation,
d) Update model values,

e) Invoke application and

f) Render response.

This page is intentionally left blank

Beans

11: What is the purpose of a *Bean* in JSF?

Answer:

Beans are similar to objects but serve different purposes. When an object is created and manipulated inside a Java program, the *Bean* calls constructors and invokes methods

12: What is the use of a Java *Bean*?

Answer:

A *Java Bean* is used mainly as a user interface builder and it is accessed by a palette window in the builder tool.

13: What is the use of a Java *Bean* in the JSF context?

Answer:

In the JSF context, a *Java Bean* is used for storing the state of web pages. Thus *Bean* creation is under the control of JSF implementation.

14: What does the JSF implementation process do?

Answer:

The JSF implementation creates and discards *Beans* when needed, reads *Bean* properties and sets the *Bean* properties when a *Form* is posted.

15: What are the properties of a *Bean* class?

Answer:

A *Bean* class needs to follow a specific set of programming conventions so that it exposes features that tools can use.

16: Which are the most important features of a *Bean*?

Answer:

The most important features of a *Bean* are the exposed properties, where properties are any of the attributes that the *Bean* has.

17: Which are the main attributes that define a *Bean*?

Answer:

The attributes that define a *Bean* are:

a) a name,
b) a type and
c) the methods for setting a value.

18: What is a Backing *Bean* in JSF?

Answer:

A *Backing Bean* is a *Bean* that contains the component objects of a web *Form*.

19: What are CDI *Beans*?

Answer:

CDI (Contexts and Dependency Injection) Beans are *Beans* that are bound to a context by the CDI that specifies mechanisms for injecting, intercepting and decorating method calls.

20: How are CDI *Beans* used in JSF?

Answer:

CDI Beans are used just as managed *Beans* are but they are declared with the *@Named* annotation.

21: What are Message Bundles in JSF?

Answer:

Message Bundles are message strings collected in a central location, simply localized and organized by JSF.

22: What are *Bean* Scopes in JSF?

Answer:

Bean Scopes are containers that hold *Beans* and other objects that need to be available in different components.

23: How many Scopes can we find in JSF?

Answer:

There are 3 types of Scope that we can find in JSF, they are:

a) The Session Scope,
b) The Request Scope and
c) The Application Scope.

JSF 2.0 adds two more scopes:

d) The View Scope and
e) The Custom Scope.

24: What does a Session Scope do in JSF?

Answer:

A *Session Scope* keeps track of the HTTP protocol, which is actually a repeated connection made by the client. This is mostly achieved using cookies.

25: What does a Request Scope do in JSF?

Answer:

A *Request Scope* is a short lived session that starts when the HTTP request is submitted and ends after a response is sent back to the client. It is often used when the storage scope is of an issue.

26: What does an Application Scope do in JSF?

Answer:

An *Application Scope* is a session that maintains itself for the duration of the web application. It is shared between all the requests and sessions.

27: What does a Conversation Scope do in JSF?

Answer:

A *Conversation Scope* ranges over a predetermined set of related pages by providing data persistence until a key goal has been reached making the storing of data for an entire session unneeded.

28: What is the purpose of a View Scope in JSF?

Answer:

The *View Scope* has been introduced in JSF. 2.0. It represents a *Bean* in the *View Scope* that persists as long as a JSF page is redisplayed. It is mainly useful for AJAX applications as it reduces the size of *Session Scopes*.

29: What does a Custom Scope do in JSF?

Answer:

A *Custom Scope* is a map that is created so that names are bound to an object, with the lifetime of a map being the reason a scope is different from another scope.

Attributes, Parameters and Tags

30: What do the *f:attribute, f: param* and *f:facet* do in JSF?

Answer:

These tags are general purpose tags that add information to a component.

31: What is the sole role of the *f:attribute* tag in JSF?

Answer:

Its role is to allow any component to store an arbitrary name or value pair in its attribute map, by allowing an attribute to be sent to page and later retrieve it programmatically.

32: What is the sole role of the *f:param* tag in JSF?

Answer:

The *f:param* tag allows for the definition of a name or pair, where the value is instead placed in a separate child component, making it a much bulkier storage mechanism than the *f:attribute* counterpart.

33: What does the *f:facet* tag do in JSF?

Answer:

This tag adds a named component to a component's facet map, where the facet components are usually rendered in a special place.

34: What does the *id attribute* allow for in JSF?

Answer:

The *id attribute* allows for accessing the JSF components from other JSF tags, obtaining component references in Java code and accessing HTML elements with scripts.

35: What does the *Converter Attribute* do in JSF?

Answer:

The *Converter Attribute* allows for the attachment of a *Converter Attribute* to a component, and in some cases allows for input tags to have a *Validator Attribute* that can be used to attach a *Validator* to a component.

36: What is the Render Attribute used for in JSF?

Answer:

The *Render Attribute* is used for the inclusion or exclusion of a component depending on a situation, such as the rendering of a Logout button if a user is logged in.

37: What are DHTML events in JSF?

Answer:

DHTML stands for *Dynamic HTML* event attributes and it represents client scripting used for many types of tasks such as syntax validation or rollover images.

38: What does the *h:panelGrid* tag do in JSF?

Answer:

The *h:panelGrid* tag uses HTML tables for layout and it is used for laying components in rows and/or columns.

39: What does the Immediate Attribute do in JSF?

Answer:

The *Immediate Attribute* is mainly used for value changes that may affect the user interface and its application is render by input components like *Menus* and *Listboxes*.

40: What does the *h:inputHidden* tag do in JSF?

Answer:

The *h:inputHidden* tag is part of the hidden fields present in JSF and it is used with JavaScript actions to send back data to the server, except that it does not support HTML and DHTML standard tags.

41: What does the *h:outputText* tag do in JSF?

Answer:

The *h:outputText* tag is the simplest of JSF tags and it is used to generate simple text with an exception: it generates an HTML span element if the style or style Class attributes are used.

42: What is the *h:outputText* tag used for in JSF?

Answer:

The *h:outpoutText* tag is used mainly for producing styled outputs, generating HTML markups and to make sure that the text is considered as a one cell of the grid in a panel grid.

43: What does the *h:graphicImage* tag do in JSF?

Answer:

The *h:graphicImage* tag is used for generating HTML img elements by specifying the image location with an URL or *Value Attribute.*

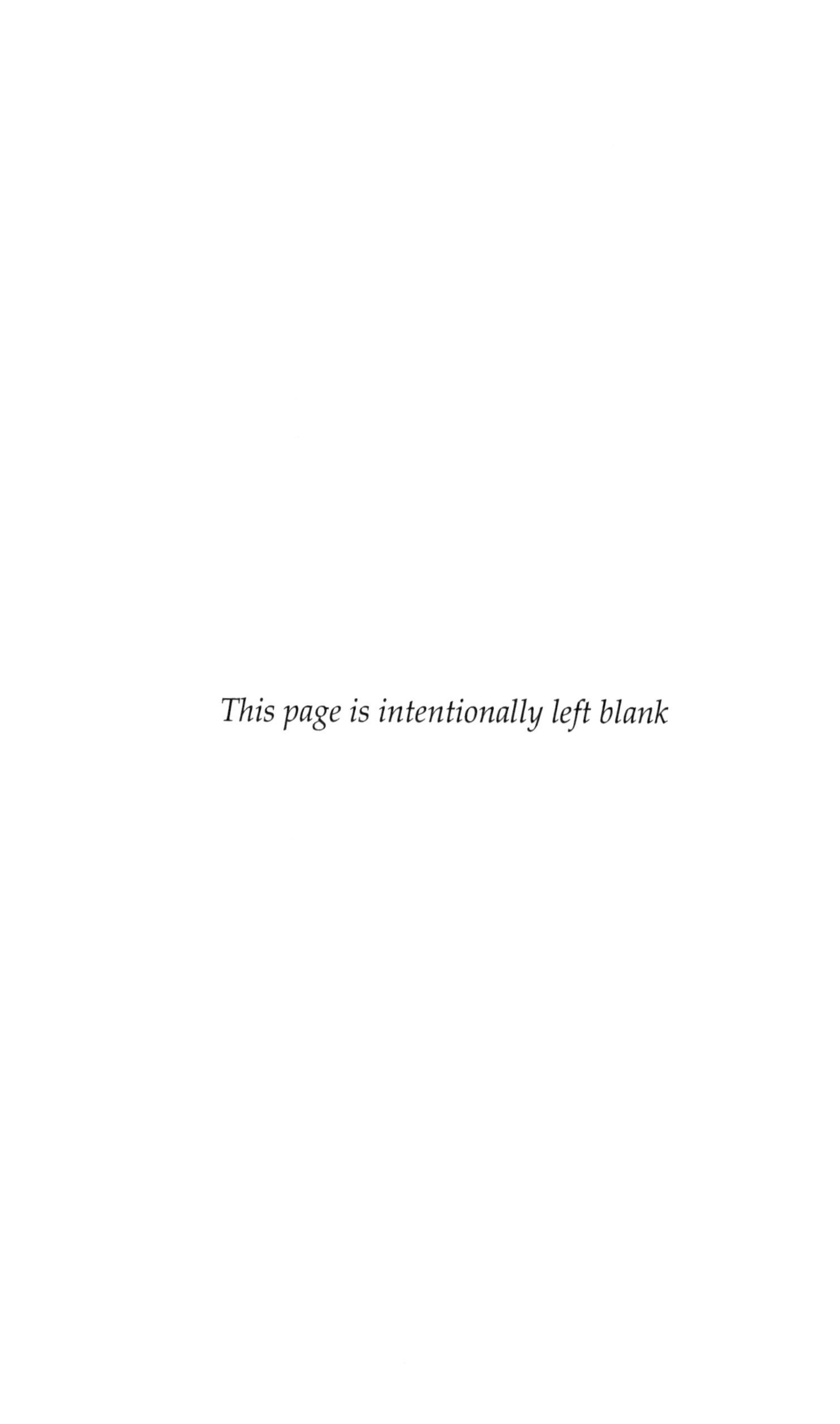
This page is intentionally left blank

Buttons, Links and Facelets

44: What are the *h:commandButton* and *h:commandLink* tags used for in JSF?

Answer:

These two tags are used to navigate within a JSF application and represent the main components of JSF navigation.

45: What does the *h:outputLink* tag do in JSF?

Answer:

This tag is used to generate HTML anchor elements to point to a resource such as a web page, with the generated link taking a user to a designated resource without the need to use JSF framework.

46: What does the *h:selectBooleanCheckbox* and *h:selectManyCheckbox* tags do in JSF?

Answer:

The first tag represents a checkbox that is wired to a *Boolean Bean* property and the second tag is used to select one or more checkboxes present in a group.

47: Which are the attributes that represent the *h:selectBooleanCheckbox* and *h:selectManyCheckbox* tags in JSF?

Answer:

There are four attributes that are unique to the two tags:

a) borde,
b) enabledClass,
c) disabledClass and
d) layout.

48: What does Border Attribute do in JSF?

Answer:

The *Border Attribute* is used to specify the width of a border, for example, radio boxes or checkboxes of the *h:select* tags.

49: What do the *enableClass* and *disableClass* attributes do in JSF?

Answer:

These two attributes are used to specify CSS classes that are used when checkboxes or radio boxes are either Enabled or Disabled.

50: What is *Facelets* in JSF?

Answer:

Facelets was designed to be an alternative to the JSP based view handler in JSF 1.1 and as of JSF 2.0 it is used to replace the default JSP view technology.

51: What are Facelets Tags used for in JSF?

Answer:

Facelets Tags are used in JSF to include content from other XHTML pages, to build pages from templates, to create custom components without the need for writing Java code and for miscellaneous utilities.

52: What does the *ui:composition* Facelet Tag do in JSF?

Answer:

The *ui:composition tag* is(when used without a template attribute) a sequence of elements which can be inserted somewhere else. When used with a template attribute, it simply allows for a template to be loaded and the children of this tag determine the variable parts of the template.

53: What does the *ui:decoration Facelet* tag do in JSF?

Answer:

This tag specifies a page where parts can be inserted, if used without a template attribute. If a template attribute is used, the children of this tag determine the variable parts of the template.

54: What does the *ui:debug Facelet* tag do in JSF?

Answer:

This tag allows for users to display a debug window, with keyboard shortcuts, that shows the component hierarchy for the currently used page and the scoped variables of the application.

55: What does the *h:dataTable* Tag do in JSF?

Answer:

The *h:dataTable* Tag is used to iterate over data to create an HTML table with value attributes such as Java Objects, Arrays or Instances of *java.util.List* and more.

56: Which tags are found in the body of a *h:dataTable* tag in JSF?

Answer:

The body of this tag can only contain *h:column* tags, with the rest of other component tags being ignored by *h:dataTable,* with each column containing an unlimited number of components.

57: What does the dir attribute of *h:dataTable* do in JSF?

Answer:

This attribute shows the text direction for the text that does not inherit directionality and provides valid values such as LTR and RTL.

58: What does the frame attribute of *h:dataTable* do in JSF?

Answer:

This attribute provides specifications for sides of the frame that surround the table such as:

a) none,

b) above,
c) below,
d) hsides,
e) vsides,
f) lhs,
g) rhs,
h) box,
i) border.

59: What does the row attribute of *h:dataTable* do in JSF?

Answer:

This attribute provides the number of rows that are displayed in the table. Starting with the row specified with the first attribute; when the value is set to 0 then all the rows of the table are displayed.

60: What styles does *h:dataTable* have in JSF?

Answer:

The *h:dataTable* tag has four attributes that specify CSS classes for the table as a whole, individual columns or rows and headers and footers.

61: What does the *ui:repeat* tag do in JSF?

Answer:

The *ui:repeat* tag may be used instead of the *h:dataTable* tag and it inserts its body into the page repeatedly by using attributes for iteration over a subset of a particular collection.

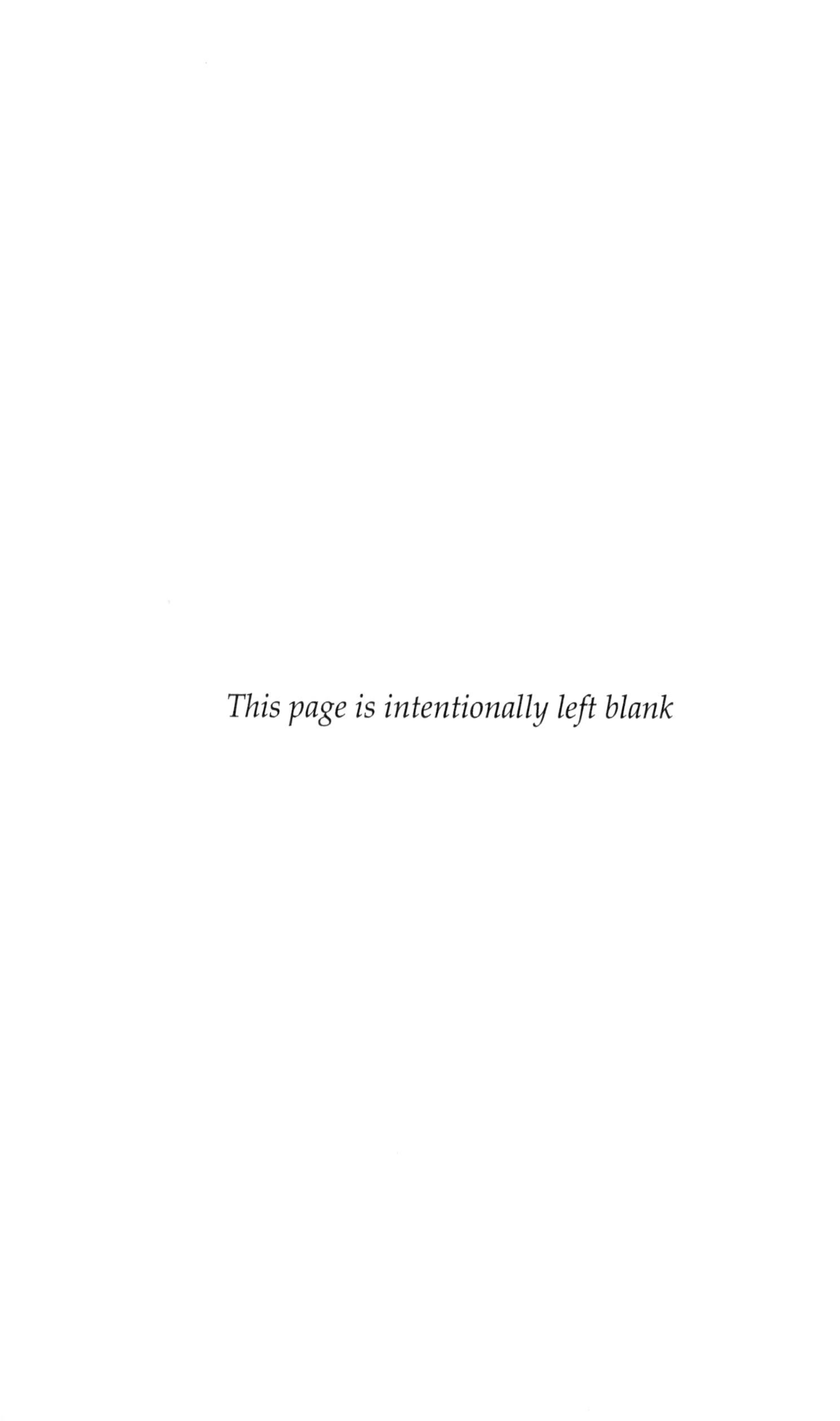

This page is intentionally left blank

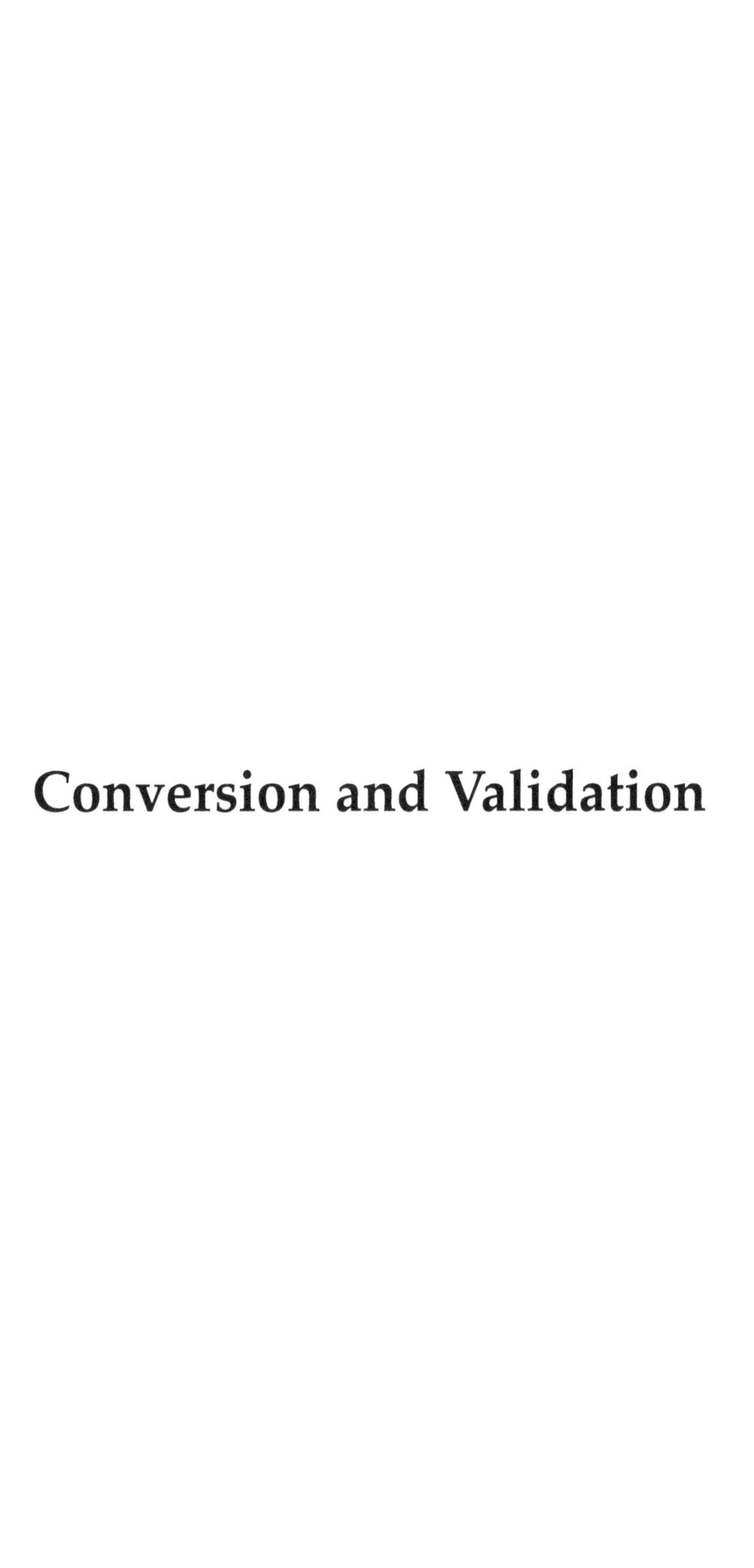

Conversion and Validation

62: What is Request Value in JSF?

Answer:

The *Request Values* represents the process of storing the requested values in component objects resulted when a user clicks the submit button and the browser sends the value to the server through an HTTP request.

63: What does the *f:convertNumber* tag do in JSF?

Answer:

This tag is one of the standard converters supplied by the JSF implementation and it is used by implementing one of the ten attributes it has at its disposal.

64: What happens when Conversion Error occurs in JSF?

Answer:

When a *Conversion Error* occurs, JSF takes two specific actions:

a) The component whose conversion failed posts a message and continues to declare itself invalid,
b) JSF redisplays the current page with values that the user provided.

65: How can an error message be displayed in JSF?

Answer:

This can be achieved by adding the *h:message* tag when converters and validators are used, so that error messages are displayed next to the components that have reported them.

66: How can JSF converters (besides *DateTimeConverter* and *NumberConverter*) be used?

Answer:

Other converters can be used by making sure that the component that uses the converter has its value bound to a backing *Bean*; Referring to a converter by class using the component tag's converter attributes or by its ID using the *converterID* attribute.

67: What does the *ConvertDateTime* tag do in JSF?

Answer:

This tag is used to convert the data of a component to a *java.util.Date* by placing it inside the component tag. It has *six attributes* that allow it to specify the type and format of the data.

68: What does the *dateStyle* attribute do in JSF?|

Answer:

This attribute defines the format specified by the *java.text.DateFormat* of the date and it is only applied if *type* is date and the *pattern* is not defined.

69: What does the Locale Attribute do in JSF?

Answer:

This attribute specifies the *locale* whose predefined styles for *dates* and *times* are used for and during formatting and/or parsing.

70: What does the Pattern Attribute do in JSF?

Answer:

This attribute is used for custom formatting patterns that determine how the *date* and *tie* string have to be formatted and parsed. If this attribute is specified, then *dateStyle* and *timeStyle* attributes are ignored.

71: What does the *timeStyle* Attribute do in JSF?

Answer:

The *timeStyle Attribute* is used to define the format as specified by *java.text.DateFormat* of a time or time part of a string. It is only applied if *type* is *time* and the *pattern* is *undefined.*

72: What does the Type Attribute do in JSF?

Answer:

This attribute specifies if the string value contains a *date, time or both.* The valid values are *date, time or both* and if no value is specified then *date* is used as default.

73: What does the *NumberConverter* tag do in JSF?

Answer:

This tag is used to convert a components data to *java.lang.Number* by placing the *convertNumber* tag inside the component tag. It has several attributes used to specify the format and type of data.

74: How can a Listener be registered on components in JSF?

Answer:

A *Listener Class* can be implemented on a component by placing a *ValueChangeListener* tag or an *ActionListener* tag within the component's page.

75: How can an author reference the backing *Bean* methods in JSF?

Answer:

An *Author* can call these methods by using the component tags *valuechangerListener* and *actionListener* attributes.

76: How can a value-changer listener be registered on a component in JSF?

Answer:

This can be achieved by having the author register a *ValueChangeListener* on a *UIInput* component or a component represented by one of the classes of the *UIInput*.

77: How can an Action Listener be registered on a component in JSF?

Answer:

An *Author* can register an *ActionListener* on a *UICommand* component by nesting an *ActionListener* tag in the component's tag of that particular page.

78: What is the purpose of the *DoubleRangeValidator* class in JSF?

Answer:

This class is used to check if the local value of a component is in a certain range, where the value of the component must be in floating point or at least convertible to a floating point.

79: What does the *LengthValidator* class do in JSF?

Answer:

This class checks if the length of a component's local value is within range and that the value is a *java.lang.String*.

80: What does *LongRangeValidator* class do in JSF?

Answer:

This class makes sure that the local value of a component is in a certain range and that the value is any *Numeric* type or *String* which can be converted to a *Long*.

81: How can a Component Value be bound to a property in JSF?

Answer:

This can be achieved by specifying the name of the *Bean* and also the name of the property that is using the value attribute, where the name of the *Bean* in the value-binding expression must match the managed *Bean* name element.

82: How can a Component Instance be bound to a *Bean* property in JSF?

Answer:

A *Component Instance* can be bound to a *Bean* property by using a value binding expression with the binding attribute of the component's tag. Most of the time, a component instance is bound rather than its value to a *Bean* property.

83: How can a backing *Bean* method be referenced in JSF?

Answer:

This can be done by having a *Component Tag* that has a set of attributes used for referencing backing *Bean* methods that can achieve certain functions for the component associated with the tag.

84: How many attributes referencing backing *Bean*

methods exist in JSF?

Answer:

There are four methods:

a) action
b) actionListener,
c) validator &
d) valueChangeListener.

85: How is a method that performs navigation referenced in JSF?

Answer:

If a page includes a component that causes the application to navigate to another page when the component is activated, the tag corresponding to this component must include an *Action Attribute.*

86: How is a method that handles an Action Event referenced in JSF?

Answer:

If a component on a certain page generates an action event, where that event is handled by a backing *Bean* method, then the method is referred to by using the component's *actionListener* attribute.

87: How is a method that performs validation referenced in JSF?

Answer:

If the input of one of the components on a page is validated by a backing *Bean* method, then the referencing is done to the method from the component's tag using the *Validation Attribute.*

88: How is a method that handles a value -change event referenced in JSF?

Answer:

If the desire is to have a component on a certain page generate *value-change events* and it is desired for that event to be handled by a backing *Bean* method, then it is referred to the method by using the component's *valueChangeListener* attribute.

89: How is a Custom Converter applied in JSF?

Answer:

A *Custom Converter* is applied to a component by either nesting a converter tag inside the component's tag or by using the converter's tag attribute.

90: How is a Custom Validator applied in JSF?

Answer:

A *Custom Validator* is applied to a component by nesting a *validator tag* or the *validator's custom tag* inside the component's tag. A *custom tag* is used by applying the *custom tag* associated with the component.

91: How can a Custom Component be used in JSF?

Answer:

A *Custom Component* can be used in page by declaring the tag library that defines the custom tag that renders the *custom component*.

Event Handling

92: How many types of events are supported by JSF?

Answer:

JSF supports four kinds of events, they are:

a) Value Change Events,
b) Action Events,
c) Phase Events &
d) System Events (since JSF 2.0).

93: How can Event Listeners affect the JSF life cycle?

Answer:

Event Listeners can affect the JSF life cycle in one of three ways:

a) By letting the cycle proceed normally,
b) By calling the render *Response Method* to skip the rest of the life cycle or
c) By calling the *responseComplete* method of the *FacesContext* class to pass by the rest of the life cycle entirely.

94: What do Value Change events do in JSF?

Answer:

Value Change events are summoned to keep dependent components in sync, by firing input components after their value has been validated.

95: How are Action Events activated in JSF?

Answer:

Action Events are fired by buttons and/or links during the Invoke Application phase when the life cycle is almost at the end.

96: What is the use of the *f:param* tag during event handling?

Answer:

The *f:param* tag is used to allow attaching of a parameter to a component, with the parameter interpreted depending on the type of component to which it is attached.

97: What is the use of the *f:attribute* tag during event handling?

Answer:

The *f:attribute* tag is used as another way to pass information from the *UI* to the *server*, by setting the tag to an attribute or a link or to switch from an action to an action listener.

98: What are Phase Events in JSF?

Answer:

Phase Events are events that are fired before and after each life cycle phase, that are handled by phase listeners and are attached to the view root.

99: How are Phase Listeners implemented in JSF?

Answer:

Phase Listeners are implemented by using the *PhaseListener* interface from the *javax.faces.event* package and by defining three methods:

a) PhaseID getPhaseID ( );
b) void afterPhase (PhaseEvent) and
c) void beforePhase (PhaseEvent).

100: How can a Listener class handle an action event?

Answer:

A *Listener Class* must implement the *javax.faces.event ActionListener* interface. It must also include the method known as *processAction (ActionEvent ActionEvent),* which is the method that is invoked when the Action Event occurs.

Composite Components

101: What does the Interface Component tag do in JSF?

Answer:

The *Interface Component* tag contains other composite tags that expose a composite component's attributes, action sources, value holders, facets and more.

102: What does the Implementation Component tag do in JSF?

Answer:

The *Implementation Tag* contains the XHTML markup that defines the component and inside the Implementation Tag the component author can easily access attributes with the expression # *{cc.attrs.attributeName}*.

103: What does the Attribute Component Tag do in JSF?

Answer:

The *Attribute Component Tag* is used in the interface section of JSF and its sole purpose is to expose an attribute of a component to the page authors.

104: What does the *valueHolder* component tag do in JSF?

Answer:

This tag is used in the interface section of JSF and it is used for exposing a component that holds value to the page authors.

105: What does the *editableValueHolder* component tag do in JSF?

Answer:

The *editableValueHolder* tag is used to expose a component that holds an editable value to the page authors. It may be accessed in the JSF interface.

106: What does the *actionSource* Component tag do in JSF?

Answer:

This tags purpose is to expose a component that fires action events like buttons and links to the page authors.

107: What does Extension Component tag do in JSF?

Answer:

The *Extension* tag is used by the author that wishes to place this tag inside any element in the interface. It can also contain an arbitrary XML and is used in the JSF interface sub element.

108: What do the *renderFacet* and *insertFacet* component tags do in JSF?

Answer:

These tags are used to *render* and *insert* a facet that is specified by the author, as a facet of the enclosing component. They are used in the JSF implementation.

109: What are Facets used for in JSF?

Answer:

Facets are used by page authors to add functionality to their components if these component users need to supply content in addition to the child components.

110: What are the requirements for a Backing Component in JSF?

Answer:

A *Backing Component* has three requirements:

a) To be a subclass of the *UIComponent,*
b) To implement the *NamingContainer* marker interface and
c) To have a family property with a value *javax.faces.NamingContainer*.

111: How are Composite Components packed in JARs and why?

Answer:

Composite Components are placed along with the style sheets, JavaScript and properties files under a META-INF directory in JAR. This is mainly used so that other developers can use these components.

112: What is the main purpose of using Composite Components in JSF?

Answer:

Composite Components are mostly used to give the JSF developers the ability to implement in a more easy to use manner of custom components that encapsulate AJAX.

113: How can AJAX be accessed in JSF?

Answer:

Since JSF 2.0 AJAX is represented as a built in support feature with JavaScript libraries and it can be accessed in both views and Java code.

114: How can AJAX use cases be handled from within JSF?

Answer:

AJAX use cases can be handled with the *f:ajax* tag, which attaches a behavior to any components, from the JSF's core library. Examples include field validations or progress indicators.

115: How do AJAX requests differ from other HTTP requests?

Answer:

AJAX requests differ in two ways:

a) The first difference is that AJAX partially processes forms on the server during the AJAX call.
b) The second difference is that it partially renders

DOM (Document Object Model) elements on the client after AJAX calls return from the server.

116: How can JSF AJAX be defined?

Answer:

JSF AJAX requests partially process components on the server and partially renders components on the client when the request returns.

117: How is the JSF life cycle split?

Answer:

As of JSF 2.0 the life cycle is split into 2 parts:

a) Execute (which is when components are executed) and
b) Render (which are the components that are rendered).

The JSF life cycle will always execute components first and then render them.

118: What happens when JSF executes components on a server?

Answer:

When JSF executes a component on a server, three processes take place:

a) JSF converts and validates the component's value,
b) Then pushes valid input values to the model and

c) Executes actions and action listeners.

119: How can AJAX be used with JSF 2.0?

Answer:

To use AJAX with JSF 2.0 there are three steps that have to be followed:

a) To associate a component and an event with an AJAX request,
b) To identify components to execute on the server and
c) To identify components those are to be rendered after an AJAX request.

120: What does the Event Attribute of the *f:ajax* tag do in JSF?

Answer:

This attribute is used to trigger the AJAX request. Event names are generally JavaScript event names without the on prefix.

121: What does the Execute Attribute of the *f:ajax* tag do in JSF?

Answer:

This attribute enables a separate list of components that JSF executes on the server during the AJAX call with valid keywords such as *@this, @form, @none, @all* and more. If the execute attribute is not specified, then the *@this* keyword is used by default.

122: What does the Onevent Attribute of the *f:ajax* tag do in JSF?

Answer:

This is a JavaScript function that JSF calls for AJAX events; it is always called three times during the lifetime of an AJAX call (begin, complete and success).

123: What does the Listener Attribute of the *f:ajax* tag do in JSF:

Answer:

JSF invokes this method once every AJAX call in the Invoke Application phase of the life cycle, which is at the end of the execute portion of the life cycle.

124: What does the Render Attribute of the *f:ajax* tag do in JSF?

Answer:

This attribute is used to generate a space separated list of component that JSF renders on the client after AJAX calls are returned from the server. If the render attribute is not specified then the default is set to *@none* and JSF will not render any components after the AJAX request completes.

125: How are Events named in JSF?

Answer:

JSF strips away the leading *on* from events such as the JavaScript *onblur* event which thus becomes *blur* or *onkeyup* leads to *keyup,* and so on.

126: What does the Complete Data Object attribute do in JSF?

Answer:

When a successful call is made, JSF uses the *Data Object Attribute* to execute portions of a life cycle before the render stage of the cycle.

127: What does the *responseXML* attribute do in JSF?

Answer:

This attribute is used to find the response to the AJAX request. This object is undefined during the begin phase of the actual AJAX request.

128: What does the *responseText* attribute do in JSF?

Answer:

This method is used to have the XML response as a text. This object is always undefined in the begin phase of the AJAX request.

129: What does the *reponseCode* attribute do in JSF?

Answer:

This attribute allows for the numeric response code of the AJAX request to be displayed. This object is undefined during the begin phase of the AJAX request.

130: How are AJAX errors handled in JSF?

Answer:

AJAX errors are handled using the *f:ajax onerror* attribute which is written like this: *<f:ajax onerror="handleAjaxError"* />.

131: Which are the properties of the data object in charge of errors?

Answer:

The *Data Object* has three attributes that are not present for events. They are:

a) *description,*
b) *errorName* and
c) *errorMessage.*

132: What are AJAX responses in JSF?

Answer:

These responses are related to the JSF AJAX requests in an XML document that instructs JSF on how to update the XHTML page from which the response was launched.

133: What does the Insert Response element do in JSF AJAX?

Answer:

This element inserts a *DOM* element with a specified *ID* before an existing element. This can be acheived as follows:

<insert id="insert id" before="before id">

<! [CDATA [...]]>

</insert>

134: What does the Update Response element do in JSF AJAX?

Answer:

This element is used to update a *DOM* element and in addition to specifying a client ID of a DOM element to update, it makes sure to either update the whole *DOM,* update the entire state of a submitting *Form* or to update the body of a page.

135: What does the delete response element do in JSF AJAX?

Answer:

This element is used to delete a DOM element with a specified ID and it is introduced as follows:

<delete id="delete id">

<! [CDATA [...]]>

</attribute>

136: What does the attributes response element do in JSF AJAX?

Answer:

The attributes element is used to update one or more attributes of the *DOM* element:

<attributes id="element id">

<attribute name="attribute name" value="attribute value"/>

...

</attribute>

137: What does the error response element do in JSF AJAX?

Answer:

This element simply generates a server error with the enclosed name and message.

138: What does the *addOnError (callback)* function do in JSF?

Answer:

This function is a JavaScript function that JSF invokes when an AJAX call results in an error.

139: What does the *addOnEvent (callback)* function do in JSF?

Answer:

This function is a JavaScript function that JSF calls for AJAX events. It is called three times throughout the lifetime of a successful AJAX call: begin, complete and success.

140: What does the *request()* method do in JSF?

Answer:

This method is used to send an AJAX requests to the server. The request is always asynchronous, queued with other AJAX requests and it is a POST to the surrounding *Form*'s action.

141: How does JSF handle queuing events?

Answer:

JSF automatically queues AJAX requests and executes them in a serial manner so that the last AJAX request is always finished before the next one has started.

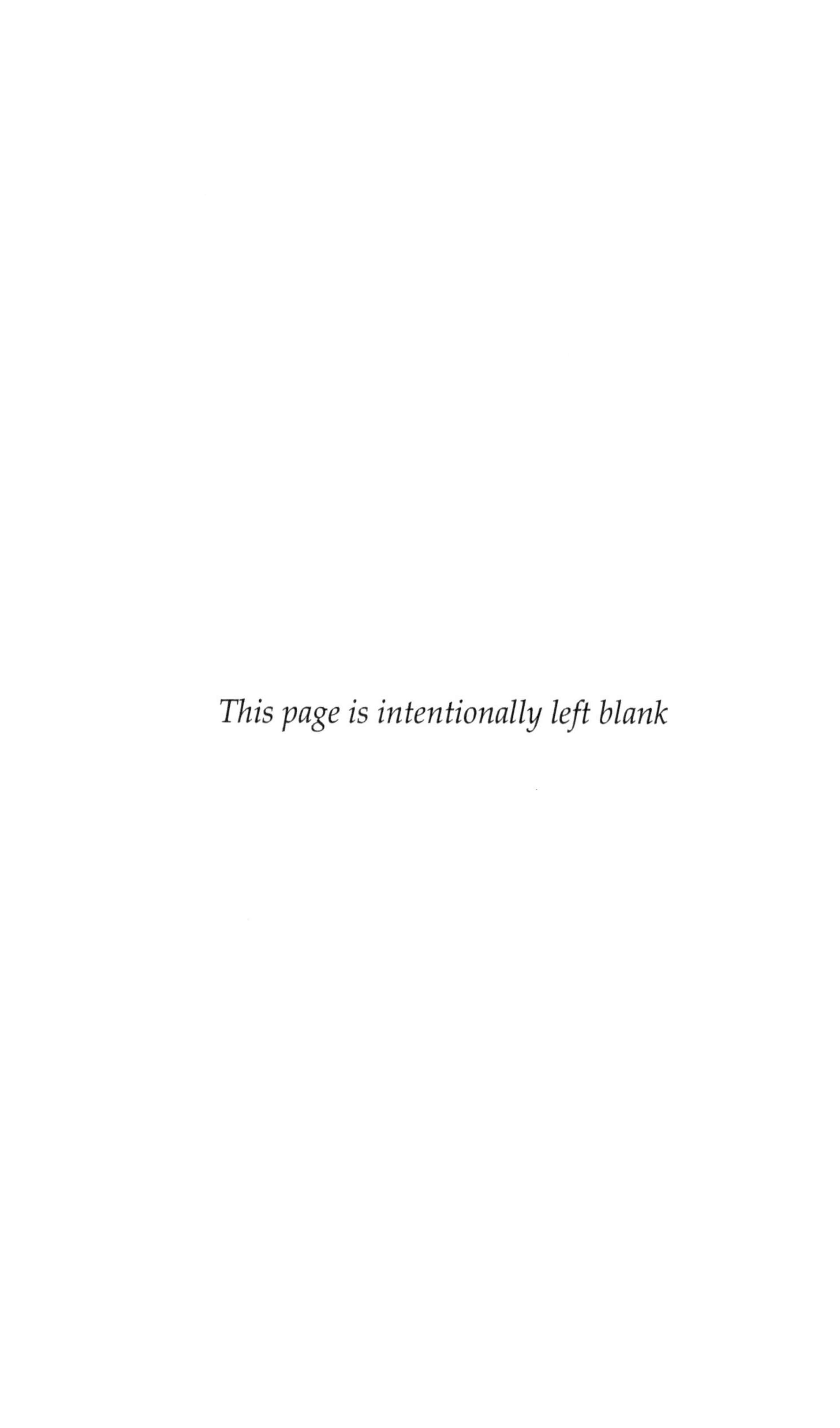

This page is intentionally left blank

Custom Components and Converters

142: Which are the responsibilities needed for a Component Class?

Answer:

A component class needs to have three responsibilities:

a) To maintain the component state,
b) To encode the user interface by writing markup and
c) To decode HTTP requests.

143: What does the *UIComponent* class manage in JSF?

Answer:

This class manages child components and a map of facet components, attributes, value expressions and a collection of event listeners.

144: How do Components Encode Markup in JSF?

Answer:

Components Encode Markup using three methods and these are:

a) encodeBegin(),
b) encodeChildren() and
c) encodeEnd().

145: What does the *ResponseWriter* class do in JSF?

Answer:

This class is used to *Write* and *Markup*. It also has

convenience methods used for starting and ending HTML elements and for writing element attributes.

146: What do the *startElement* and *endElement* methods do in JSF?

Answer:

These methods produce the element delimiters and keep track of child elements so that the author does not have to worry with input distinctions.

147: What does the *writeAttribute* method do in JSF?

Answer:

The *writeAttribute* method is used to write an attribute name or attribute value pair with the appropriate escape characters.

148: What does the String *getClientID (FacesContext context)* method do in JSF?

Answer:

This method is used to return a client ID for the *FaceContext* component, where the JSF framework creates the client ID from the ID of the enclosing *Form* and the ID of this component.

149: What is the *Map<String, Object>* Attributes method used for in JSF?

Answer:

This method is used to return a mutable map of component attributes and also properties. It is used to *view, add, update* and *remove* attributes from a component.

150: What does the *ResponseWriter getResponseWriter ()* method do in JSF?

Answer:

This method is used to return a reference to the response writer. The author can easily plug his own response writer into the JSF.

151: What does the *void startElement (String elementName, UIComponent component)* method do in JSF?

Answer:

This method is used to write the start tag for a specified element, with a component parameter that allows tools to associate a component and its markup. At the moment, the JSF reference implementation ignores this attribute.

152: What does the *void writeAttribute(String attributeName, String attributeValue, String componentProperty)* method do in JSF?

Answer:

This method is used to write the value of an attribute. It

can only be called between calls to *startElement*() and *endElement*(). This method is not used by the JSF reference implementation.

153: What does the *void decode (FacesContext context)* method do in JSF?

Answer:

This method is called by JSF at the beginning of the JSF life cycle only if the components renderer type is *NULL,* which means that *component renders itself.*

154: What does the *ExternalContext getExternalContext()* method do in JSF?

Answer:

This method is used to return a reference to a context proxy, where the context is *servlet* or *portlet* context.

155: What does the *Map getRequestParameterMap()* method do in JSF?

Answer:

This method returns a map of the request parameters. Custom components usually call this method in *decode()* to check if they were the component that triggered the request.

156: What does the *void setSubmittedValue(Object*

***submittedValue)* method do in JSF?**

Answer:

This method is used to set a component's submitted value and input values. The submit value is a value that the user enters, most of the times in a web page.

157: What does the *getRendersChildren* method do in JSF?

Answer:

This method specifies if a renderer is responsible for the rendition of its component's children. If it returns as *FALSE* then JSF will not call that method and the children will always be encoded separately.

158: What does the *convertClientId* method do in JSF?

Answer:

This method is mainly used to convert an *ID* string in a way that allows for the clients to place restrictions on *IDs*, like limiting the use of special characters of numbers.

159: What does the *getConvertedValue* method do in JSF?

Answer:

This method converts a component's submitted value from a string to a simple object, with the default implementation in the Renderer class returning the submitted value.

160: What does the Converter *createConverter(Class targetClass)* method do in JSF?

Answer:

This method is used to create a converter by following its given target class; JSF implementations maintain a map of valid converter types that the author has to name in a faces file.

161: What does the *UIComponent getFacet(String facetName)* method do in JSF?

Answer:

This method is used to return references to the facets, but only if these exist. If facets do not exist, then the method is returned as *NULL*.

162: What does the *boolean getRendersChildren()* method do in JSF?

Answer:

This method returns as *TRUE* if the component renders its children and *FALSE* if it does not. It is by default set to return this value as *FALSE*.

163: What does the *boolean isRendered()* method do in JSF?

Answer:

This method simply returns the rendered property that

the author specifies, with the component being rendered only if the property is true.

164: What does the *void restoreState(FacesContext context, Object state)* method do in JSF?

Answer:

This method restores the state of this object from the given state object which is a copy of an object that has been previously obtained from calling *saveState*.

165: How is AJAX functionality added to custom components?

Answer:

This process can be achieved in two ways:

a) By embedding AJAX into a custom component or
b) By AJAX-enabling custom components to support the *f:ajax* tag.

166: What is a Tag Handler and what does it do in JSF?

Answer:

A *Tag Handler* is used to process tag attributes and their values. It uses special rules if the attribute is a special value, or, if there is a property setter for the attribute used to call it.

167: What does the *String getRemoteUser()* method do in

JSF?

Answer:

This method is used to get the name of the user that is logged in at the moment of query and it is returned as *NULL* if no such user exists.

168: What does the *Boolean isUserInRole(String role)* method do in JSF?

Answer:

This method is mainly used to test if the current user belongs to any of the given role and it is part of *javax.servlet.HTTPServeletRequest* string.

This page is intentionally left blank

How to?

169: How are files uploaded in JSF?

Answer:

Because JSF does not directly support file encoding, the author needs to install a server filter that intercepts the uploaded files and turns them into request attributes or all other *Form* data into request parameters.

170: How many attributes does the Upload Component support in JSF?

Answer:

The *Upload Component* supports two attributes in JSF and they are *value* and *target*.

The *value* attribute is used to denote a value expression into which the file contents are stored.

The *target* attribute is used to specify the target location of the file.

171: What does the Decode Method of the upload component do in JSF?

Answer:

This method retrieves file items that the servlet filter places into request attributes and disposes them as directed by the tag attributes.

172: How is an Image Map shown in JSF?

Answer:

The author needs to implement a *Client Side Image Map* that is supplied by the *usemap* attribute, where the author specifies the map in HTML in the JSF page.

173: How is Binary Data produced in JSF?

Answer:

Because it is difficult to have JSF dynamically produce *Binary Data* such an image or PDF file, the author needs to provide a JSF tag that gathers customization data that is then sent to a servlet.

174: How can binary data be generated in JSF without the use of a servlet?

Answer:

This can be achieved by having the author pay attention to the timing of servlet output stream grabbing before the JSF implementation begins writing the response.

175: When does the Filter Action take place in JSF?

Answer:

The *Filter Action* can only take place when view *IDs* that start with */binary* are present and just as servlet solutions, the filter action needs to have a data transfer object included as a *GET* parameter.

176: What is a Pager in JSF?

Answer:

A *Pager* is a standard user interface used to navigate a large table, a set of links to another page of the table, to the next and previous pages and more.

177: What does the Encode Method do in JSF?

Answer:

The *Encode Method* is used to generate sets of links; similar to the *commandLink* method. Clicking the links goes to activate JavaScript code that then sets a value in hidden field. and lastly submits the *Form*.

178: How is pop-up window generated in JSF?

Answer:

To generate *pop-up windows* the author needs to use JavaScript calls that makes sure the window is displayed when the user clicks a button or a link. The author also has to attach a function to the *onclick handler* of the button or the link and also to set the function return *FALSE* so that the browser does not submit the *Form* or follow the link.

179: What does the *doPopup* function do in JSF?

Answer:

The *doPopup* function contains the JavaScript instructions for popping up the window and it is contained in a script tag that is inside the page header.

180: How can parts of a page be shown or hidden in JSF?

Answer:

This process can be achieved using *JSTL c:if* and *c:choose* construct methods; if the author does not wish to mix JSF and JSTL tags, JSF can be used to achieve the same effect by using the *render* property.

181: What is the *getErrorMessage* method used for in JSF?

Answer:

This method is used to format an error message that is to be included in the client side JavaScript code with the error code constructed from the message and the arg attributes.

182: What does the *findValidators* method do in JSF?

Answer:

This method is part of the *validatorScript* component and is used to scan the component tree, locate all the components, enumerate their *validators* and then check which one is a certain *validator* that the author looks for and then gather them in a map object.

183: How is an application configured in JSF?

Answer:

A good method is to supply configuration parameters in the *web.xml* files and to provide a set of context *param* elements inside a *web-app* element.

184: How can JSF expression language be extended?

Answer:

This can be achieved by adding a *resolver* that processes an expression such as *base, property*. Where *base* is a *string view* and *property* may be a *Form ID*.

185: How can a function be added to the JSF expression language?

Answer:

This can be achieved by having the author add its own function to the JSF expression language by:

a) Implementing the function as a static method and/or in the *Facelets* tag library file,
b) Map the function name to the implementation.

186: How can traffic between the browser and the server be monitored?

Answer:

This is usually useful for debugging AJAX based applications and the entire traffic can be monitored using *Eclipse* or *NetBeans*. A general purpose TCP/IP sniffer can also be used, like *WireShark*.

187: How can a page be debugged in JSF?

Answer:

To do this the author must make sure that the submit button is contained inside a *h:form,* double check the navigation rules and/or install a *phase tracker*.

188: How are Testing Tools used while developing a JSF application?

Answer:

It can be achieved by testing *Beans* in isolation and by calling methods that the JSF implementation would have called.

189: How can Scala be used with JSF?

Answer:

Scala can be used by implementing a managed *Bean,* annotate it as in Java, but with the *Scala* annotation syntax.

190: How can Groovy be used with JSF?

Answer:

Because almost all Java code is *Groovy legal,* it is only needed to change the suffix of the code from*.java* to *.groovy* and then use the *Groovy* compiler to compile the code to a *.class* file

191: What are the most common Outcome Strings and what do they mean?

Answer:

The *Outcome* can be anything the developer chooses, but the most common *Outcomes* are:

a) *success* meaning everything worked, go on to the next page,
b) *failure* meaning something is wrong go on to the error page,
c) *logon* meaning the user needs to log on first, go on to the logon page,
d) *no results* meaning the search did not find anything, go to the search page again.

192: What should the deployment descriptor include for a JavaServer Faces application?

Answer:

The deployment descriptor must include certain configuration about the servlet used to process JSF requests, the servlet mapping for the processing servlet and the path to the configuration resource file if it is not located in a default location. It can also specify optional configuration which include the following: verifying custom objects, turning on XML validation or specifying where component state is saved.

193: How can you turn on validation of XML files?

Answer:

In case the JSF application contains one or more xml configuration resource files, you can turn on the JSF validation for this xml files by setting the *validateXML* flag to *TRUE*. The default value for this flag is *FALSE*.

194: Which are the required JAR files needed by the JSF application in order to run properly?

Answer:

JSF applications need several JAR files to run properly. The following are the required jars:

a) jsf-api.jar,
b) jsf-impl.jar,
c) jstl.jar,
d) standard.jar,
e) commons-*Bean*utils.jar,
f) commons-digester.jar,
g) commons-collections.jar,
h) commons-logging.jar.

195: What does a *character set* represent?

Answer:

A *character set* is a set of textual and graphic symbols, each of which is mapped to a set of non-negative integers. When the encoding of the Java program source file doesn't support Unicode/ the Unicode characters can be represented as escape sequences using the notation *uXXXX*, where *XXXX* is the character's 16-bit hexadecimal representation.

196: What are some of the cutting edge open-source software that plugs into JSF?

Answer:

JSF is highly extensible and it was very attractive to framework developers. They built open-source software such as *Facelets, Ajax4jsf, Seam, RichFaces, ICEFaces*, and so on.

197: How do you find additional components for your JSF application?

Answer:

The standard JSF defines a minimal set of components. In case you need more complex components, there are several component libraries that are worth investigating: *ICEFaces, RichFaces, PrimeFaces, the Apache Trinidad library, the Apache Tomahawk library*, and so on.

198: How do you customize error pages?

Answer:

You can substitute an error page, using *error-page tag* in *web.xml* file and specifying either a Java exception class or an HTML error code. For example

<error-page>

<error-code>500</error-code>

<location>/faces/error.xhtml</location>

</error-page>

In case an exception occurs and an error page matches its type, then that page is displayed, otherwise, an HTTP error 500 is generated.

199: How can a JSF application be tested?

Answer:

Managed Beans can be tested in isolation, by calling the methods that the JSF implementation would have called in different scenarios. For this kind of tests Unit Testing and Back-Box Testing is good. Test automation frameworks as HTMLUnit or Selenium may be used to write scripts that simulate browser sessions.

200: What does Request Encoding do in JSF?

Answer:

Request Encoding is the character encoding in which parameters from an incoming request are processed and then interpreted with the default ISO-8859-1 parse data requester.

This page is intentionally left blank

HR Questions

Review these typical interview questions and think about how you would answer them. Read the answers listed; you will find best possible answers along with strategies and suggestions.

1: Tell me about yourself?

Answer:

The most often asked question in interviews. You need to have a short statement prepared in your mind. Keep your answer to one or two minutes. Don't ramble. Be careful that it does not sound rehearsed. Limit it to work-related items unless instructed otherwise. Talk about things you have done and jobs you have held that relate to the position you are interviewing for. Start with the item farthest back and work up to the present (If you have a profile or personal statement(s) at the top of your CV use this as your starting point).

2: Why did you leave your last job?

Answer:

Stay positive regardless of the circumstances. Never refer to a major problem with management and never speak ill of supervisors, co- workers or the organization. If you do, you will be the one looking bad. Keep smiling and talk about leaving for a positive reason such as an opportunity, a chance to do something special or other forward- looking reasons.

3: What experience do you have in this field?

Answer:

Speak about specifics that relate to the position you are

applying for. If you do not have specific experience, get as close as you can.

4: Do you consider yourself successful?

Answer:

You should always answer yes and briefly explain why. A good explanation is that you have set goals, and you have met some and are on track to achieve the others.

5: What do co-workers say about you?

Answer:

Be prepared with a quote or two from co-workers. Either a specific statement or a paraphrase will work. Bill Smith, a co-worker at Clarke Company, always said I was the hardest worker's he had ever known. It should be as powerful as Bill having said it at the interview herself.

6: What do you know about this organization?

Answer:

This question is one reason to do some research on the organization before the interview. Research the company's products, size, reputation, Image, goals, problems, management style, skills, History and philosophy. Be informed and interested. Find out where they have been and where they are going. What are the current issues and who are the major players?

7: What have you done to improve your knowledge in the last year?

Answer:

Try to include improvement activities that relate to the job. A wide variety of activities can be mentioned as positive self-improvement. Have some good ones handy to mention.

8: Are you applying for other jobs?

Answer:

Be honest but do not spend a lot of time in this area. Keep the focus on this job and what you can do for this organization. Anything else is a distraction.

9: Why do you want to work for this organization?

Answer:

This may take some thought and certainly, should be based on the research you have done on the organization. Sincerity is extremely important here and will easily be sensed. Relate it to your long-term career goals. Never talk about what you want; first talk about their Needs. You want to be part of an exciting forward-moving company. You can make a definite contribution to specific company goals.

10: Do you know anyone who works for us?

Answer:

Be aware of the policy on relatives working for the organization. This can affect your answer even though they asked about friends not relatives. Be careful to mention a friend
only if they are well thought of.

11: What kind of salary do you need?

Answer:

A loaded question! A nasty little game that you will probably lose if you answer first. So, do not answer it. Instead/ say something like/ that's a tough question. Can you tell me the range for this position? In most cases, the interviewer, taken off guard, will tell you. If not, say that it can depend on the details of the job. Then give a wide range.

12: Are you a team player?

Answer:

You are, of course, a team player. Be sure to have examples ready. Specifics that show you often perform for the good of the team rather than for yourself is good evidence of your team attitude. Do not brag; just say it in a matter-of-fact tone. This is a key point.

13: How long would you expect to work for us if hired?

Answer:

Specifics here are not good. Something like this should work:

I'd like it to be a long time. Or As long as we both feel I'm doing a good job.

14: Have you ever had to fire anyone? How did you feel about that?

Answer:

This is serious. Do not make light of it or in any way seem like you like to fire people. At the same time, you will do it when it is the right thing to do. When it comes to the organization versus the individual who has created a harmful situation, you will protect the organization. Remember firing is not the same as layoff or reduction in force.

15: What is your philosophy towards work?

Answer:

The interviewer is not looking for a long or flowery dissertation here. Do you have strong feelings that the job gets done? Yes. That's the type of answer that works best here. Keep it short and positive, showing a benefit to the organization.

16: If you had enough money to retire right now, would

you?

Answer:

Answer yes if you would. But since you need to work, this is the type of work you prefer. Do not say yes if you do not mean it.

17: Have you ever been asked to leave a position?

Answer:

If you have not, say no. If you have, be honest, brief and avoid saying negative things about the people or organization involved.

18: Explain how you would be an asset to this organization.

Answer:

You should be anxious for this question. It gives you a chance to highlight your best points as they relate to the position being discussed. Give a little advance thought to this relationship.

19: Why should we hire you?

Answer:

Point out how your assets meet what the organization needs. Also mention about your knowledge, experience, abilities, and skills. Never mention any other candidates to make a comparison.

20: Tell me about a suggestion you have made.

Answer:

Have a good one ready. Be sure and use a suggestion that was accepted and was then considered successful. One related to the type of work applied for is a real plus.

21: What irritates you about co-workers?

Answer:

This is a trap question. Think real hard but fail to come up with anything that irritates you. A short statement that you seem to get along with folks is great.

22: What is your greatest strength?

Answer:

Numerous answers are good, just stay positive. A few good examples: Your ability to prioritize, Your problem-solving skills, Your ability to work under pressure, Your ability to focus on projects, Your professional expertise, Your leadership skills, Your positive attitude

23: Tell me about your dream job or what are you looking for in a job?

Answer:

Stay away from a specific job. You cannot win. If you say the job you are contending for is it, you strain credibility. If you say another job is it, you plant the suspicion that you will be dissatisfied with this position if hired. The best is to stay genetic and say something like: A job where I love the work, like the people, can contribute and can't wait to get to work.

24: Why do you think you would do well at this job?

Answer:

Give several reasons and include skills, experience and interest.

25: What do you find the most attractive about this position (Least attractive)?

Answer:

a) List a couple of attractive factors such as the responsibility the post offers and the opportunity to work with experienced teams that have a reputation for innovation and creativity.
b) Say you'd need more information and time before being able to make a judgment on any unattractive aspects.

26: What kind of person would you refuse to work with?

Answer:

Do not be trivial. It would take disloyalty to the organization, violence or lawbreaking to get you to object. Minor objections will label you as a whiner.

27: What is more important to you: the money or the work?

Answer:

Money is always important, but the work is the most important. There is no better answer.

28: What would your previous supervisor say your strongest point is?

Answer:

There are numerous good possibilities:

Loyalty, Energy, Positive attitude, Leadership, Team player, Expertise, Initiative, Patience, Hard work, Creativity, Problem solver.

29: Tell me about a problem you had with a supervisor.

Answer:

Biggest trap of all! This is a test to see if you will speak ill of your boss. If you fall for it and tell about a problem with a former boss, you may well below the interview right there. Stay positive and develop a poor memory about any trouble with a supervisor.

30: What has disappointed you about a job?

Answer:

Don't get trivial or negative. Safe areas are few but can include:

Not enough of a challenge. You were laid off in a reduction Company did not win a contract, which would have given you more responsibility.

31: Tell me about your ability to work under pressure.

Answer:

You may say that you thrive under certain types of pressure. Give an example that relates to the type of position applied for.

32: Do your skills match this job or another job more closely?

Answer:

Probably this one! Do not give fuel to the suspicion that you may want another job more than this one.

33: What motivates you to do your best on the job?

Answer:

This is a personal trait that only you can say, but good examples are: Challenge, Achievement, and Recognition.

34: Are you willing to work overtime? Nights? Weekends?

Answer:

This is up to you. Be totally honest.

35: How would you know you were successful on this job?

Answer:

Several ways are good measures:

You set high standards for yourself and meet them. Your outcomes are a success. Your boss tells you that you are successful and doing a great job.

36: Would you be willing to relocate if required?

Answer:

You should be clear on this with your family prior to the interview if you think there is a chance it may come up. Do not say yes just to get the job if the real answer is no. This can create a lot of problems later on in your career. Be honest at this point. This will save you from future grief.

37: Are you willing to put the interests of the organization ahead of your own?

Answer:

This is a straight loyalty and dedication question. Do not worry about the deep ethical and philosophical implications. Just say yes.

38: Describe your management style.

Answer:

Try to avoid labels. Some of the more common labels, like progressive, salesman or consensus, can have several meanings or descriptions depending on which management expert you listen to. The situational style is safe, because it says you will manage according to the situation, instead of one size fits all.

39: What have you learned from mistakes on the job?

Answer:

Here you have to come up with something or you strain credibility. Make it small, well intentioned mistake with a positive lesson learned. An example would be, working too far ahead of colleagues on a project and thus throwing coordination off.

40: Do you have any blind spots?

Answer:

Trick question! If you know about blind spots, they are no longer blind spots. Do not reveal any personal areas of concern here. Let them do their own discovery on your bad points. Do not hand it to them.

41: If you were hiring a person for this job, what would you look for?

Answer:

Be careful to mention traits that are needed and that you

have.

42: Do you think you are overqualified for this position?

Answer:

Regardless of your qualifications, state that you are very well qualified for the position you've been interviewed for.

43: How do you propose to compensate for your lack of experience?

Answer:

First, if you have experience that the interviewer does not know about, bring that up: Then, point out (if true) that you are a hard working quick learner.

44: What qualities do you look for in a boss?

Answer:

Be generic and positive. Safe qualities are knowledgeable, a sense of humor, fair, loyal to subordinates and holder of high standards. All bosses think they have these traits.

45: Tell me about a time when you helped resolve a dispute between others.

Answer:

Pick a specific incident. Concentrate on your problem solving technique and not the dispute you settled.

46: What position do you prefer on a team working on a project?

Answer:

Be honest. If you are comfortable in different roles, point that out.

47: Describe your work ethic.

Answer:

Emphasize benefits to the organization. Things like, determination to get the job done and work hard but enjoy your work are good.

48: What has been your biggest professional disappointment?

Answer:

Be sure that you refer to something that was beyond your control. Show acceptance and no negative feelings.

49: Tell me about the most fun you have had on the job.

Answer:

Talk about having fun by accomplishing something for the organization.

50: What would you do for us? (What can you do for us that someone else can't?)

Answer:

a) Relate past experiences that represent success in Working for your previous employer.
b) Talk about your fresh perspective and the relevant experience you can bring to the company.
c) Highlight your track record of providing creative, Workable solutions.

51: Do you have any questions for me?

Answer:

Always have some questions prepared. Questions prepared where you will be an asset to the organization are good. How soon will I be able to be productive? What type of projects will I be able to assist on?

And Finally Good Luck!

INDEX

JavaServer Faces Questions

Introduction to JSF

Beans

27: What does a Conversation Scope do in JSF?

28: What is the purpose of a View Scope in JSF?

29: What does a Custom Scope do in JSF?

Attributes, Parameters and Tags

30: What do the *f:attribute, f: param* and *f:facet* do in JSF?

31: What is the sole role of the *f:attribute* tag in JSF?

32: What is the sole role of the *f:param* tag in JSF?

33: What does the *f:facet* tag do in JSF?

34: What does the *id attribute* allow for in JSF?

35: What does the *Converter Attribute* do in JSF?

36: What is the Render Attribute used for in JSF?

37: What are DHTML events in JSF?

38: What does the *h:panelGrid* tag do in JSF?

39: What does the Immediate Attribute do in JSF?

40: What does the *h:inputHidden* tag do in JSF?

41: What does the *h:outputText* tag do in JSF?

42: What is the *h:outputText* tag used for in JSF?

43: What does the *h:graphicImage* tag do in JSF?

Buttons, Links and Facelets

44: What are the *h:commandButton* and *h:commandLink* tags used for in JSF?

45: What does the *h:outputLink* tag do in JSF?

46: What does the *h:selectBooleanCheckbox* and *h:selectManyCheckbox* tags do in JSF?

47: Which are the attributes that represent the *h:selectBooleanCheckbox* and *h:selectManyCheckbox* tags in JSF?

48: What does Border Attribute do in JSF?

49: What do the *enableClass* and *disableClass* attributes do in JSF?

50: What is *Facelets* in JSF?

51: What are Facelets Tags used for in JSF?

52: What does the *ui:composition* Facelet Tag do in JSF?

53: What does the *ui:decoration Facelet* tag do in JSF?

54: What does the *ui:debug Facelet* tag do in JSF?

55: What does the *h:dataTable* Tag do in JSF?

56: Which tags are found in the body of a *h:dataTable* tag in JSF?

57: What does the dir attribute of *h:dataTable* do in JSF?

58: What does the frame attribute of *h:dataTable* do in JSF?

59: What does the row attribute of *h:dataTable* do in JSF?

60: What styles does *h:dataTable* have in JSF?

61: What does the *ui:repeat* tag do in JSF?

Conversion and Validation

62: What is Request Value in JSF?

63: What does the *f:convertNumber* tag do in JSF?

64: What happens when Conversion Error occurs in JSF?

65: How can an error message be displayed in JSF?

66: How can JSF converters (besides *DateTimeConverter* and *NumberConverter)* be used?

67: What does the *ConvertDateTime* tag do in JSF?

68: What does the *dateStyle* attribute do in JSF?

69: What does the Locale Attribute do in JSF?

70: What does the Pattern Attribute do in JSF?

71: What does the *timeStyle* Attribute do in JSF?

72: What does the Type Attribute do in JSF?

73: What does the *NumberConverter* tag do in JSF?

74: How can a Listener be registered on components in JSF?

75: How can an author reference the backing *Bean* methods in JSF?

76: How can a value-changer listener be registered on a component in JSF?

77: How can an Action Listener be registered on a component in JSF?

78: What is the purpose of the *DoubleRangeValidator* class in JSF?

79: What does the *LengthValidator* class do in JSF?

80: What does *LongRangeValidator* class do in JSF?

81: How can a Component Value be bound to a property in JSF?

82: How can a Component Instance be bound to a *Bean* property in JSF?

83: How can a backing *Bean* method be referenced in JSF?

84: How many attributes referencing backing *Bean* methods exist in JSF?

85: How is a method that performs navigation referenced in JSF?

86: How is a method that handles an Action Event referenced in

87: How is a method that performs validation referenced in JSF?

88: How is a method that handles a value-change event referenced in JSF?

89: How is a Custom Converter applied in JSF?

90: How is a Custom Validator applied in JSF?

91: How can a Custom Component be used in JSF?

Event Handling

92: How many types of events are supported by JSF?

93: How can Event Listeners affect the JSF life cycle?

94: What do Value Change events do in JSF?

95: How are Action Events activated in JSF?

96: What is the use of the *f:param* tag during event handling?

97: What is the use of the *f:attribute* tag during event handling?

98: What are Phase Events in JSF?

99: How are Phase Listeners implemented in JSF?

100: How can a Listener class handle an action event?

Composite Components

101: What does the Interface Component tag do in JSF?

102: What does the Implementation Component tag do in JSF?

103: What does the Attribute Component Tag do in JSF?

104: What does the *valueHolder* component tag do in JSF?

105: What does the *editableValueHolder* component tag do in JSF?

106: What does the *actionSource* Component tag do in JSF?

107: What does Extension Component tag do in JSF?

108: What do the *renderFacet* and *insertFacet* component tags do in JSF?

109: What are Facets used for in JSF?

110: What are the requirements for a Backing Component in JSF?

111: How are Composite Components packed in JARs and why?

112: What is the main purpose of using Composite Components in JSF?

113: How can AJAX be accessed in JSF?

114: How can AJAX use cases be handled from within JSF?

115: How do AJAX requests differ from other HTTP requests?

116: How can JSF AJAX be defined?

117: How is the JSF life cycle split?

118: What happens when JSF executes components on a server?

119: How can AJAX be used with JSF 2.0?

120: What does the Event Attribute of the *f:ajax* tag do in JSF?

121: What does the Execute Attribute of the *f:ajax* tag do in JSF?

122: What does the Onevent Attribute of the *f:ajax* tag do in JSF?

123: What does the Listener Attribute of the *f:ajax* tag do in JSF:

124: What does the Render Attribute of the *f:ajax* tag do in JSF?

125: How are Events named in JSF?

126: What does the Complete Data Object attribute do in JSF?

127: What does the *responseXML* attribute do in JSF?

128: What does the *responseText* attribute do in JSF?

129: What does the *reponseCode* attribute do in JSF?

130: How are AJAX errors handled in JSF?

131: Which are the properties of the data object in charge of errors?

132: What are AJAX responses in JSF?

133: What does the Insert Response element do in JSF AJAX?

134: What does the Update Response element do in JSF AJAX?

135: What does the delete response element do in JSF AJAX?

136: What does the attributes response element do in JSF AJAX?

137: What does the error response element do in JSF AJAX?

138: What does the *addOnError (callback)* function do in JSF?

139: What does the *addOnEvent (callback)* function do in JSF?

140: What does the *request()* method do in JSF?

141: How does JSF handle queuing events?

Custom Components and Converters

142: Which are the responsibilities needed for a Component Class?

143: What does the *UIComponent* class manage in JSF?

144: How do Components Encode Markup in JSF?

145: What does the *ResponseWriter* class do in JSF?

146: What do the *startElement* and *endElement* methods do in JSF?

147: What does the *writeAttribute* method do in JSF?

148: What does the String *getClientID (FacesContext context)* method do in JSF?

149: What is the *Map<String, Object>* Attributes method used for in JSF?

150: What does the *ResponseWriter getResponseWriter ()* method do in JSF?

151: What does the *void startElement (String elementName, UIComponent component)* method do in JSF?

152: What does the *void writeAttribute(String attributeName, String attributeValue, String componentProperty)* method do in JSF?

153: What does the *void decode (FacesContext context)* method do in JSF?

154: What does the *ExternalContext getExternalContext()* method do in JSF?

155: What does the *Map getRequestParameterMap()* method do in JSF?

156: What does the *void setSubmittedValue(Object submittedValue)* method do in JSF?

157: What does the *getRendersChildren* method do in JSF?

158: What does the *convertClientId* method do in JSF?

159: What does the *getConvertedValue* method do in JSF?

160: What does the Converter *createConverter(Class targetClass)* method do in JSF?

161: What does the *UIComponent getFacet(String facetName)* method do in JSF?

162: What does the *boolean getRendersChildren()* method do in JSF?

163: What does the *boolean isRendered()* method do in JSF?

164: What does the *void restoreState(FacesContext context, Object state)* method do in JSF?

165: How is AJAX functionality added to custom components?

166: What is a Tag Handler and what does it do in JSF?

167: What does the *String getRemoteUser()* method do in JSF?

168: What does the *Boolean isUserInRole(String role)* method do in JSF?

How to?

169: How are files uploaded in JSF?

170: How many attributes does the Upload Component support in JSF?

171: What does the Decode Method of the upload component do in JSF?

172: How is an Image Map shown in JSF?

173: How is Binary Data produced in JSF?

174: How can binary data be generated in JSF without the use of a servlet?

175: When does the Filter Action take place in JSF?

176: What is a Pager in JSF?

177: What does the Encode Method do in JSF?

178: How is pop-up window generated in JSF?

179: What does the *doPopup* function do in JSF?

180: How can parts of a page be shown or hidden in JSF?

181: What is the *getErrorMessage* method used for in JSF?

182: What does the *findValidators* method do in JSF?

183: How is an application configured in JSF?

184: How can JSF expression language be extended?

185: How can a function be added to the JSF expression language?

186: How can traffic between the browser and the server be monitored?

187: How can a page be debugged in JSF?

188: How are Testing Tools used while developing a JSF application?

189: How can Scala be used with JSF?

190: How can Groovy be used with JSF?

191: What are the most common Outcome Strings and what do they mean?

192: What should the deployment descriptor include for a JavaServer Faces application?

193: How can you turn on validation of XML files?

194: Which are the required JAR files needed by the JSF application in order to run properly?

195: What does a *character set* represent?

196: What are some of the cutting edge open-source software that plugs into JSF?

197: How do you find additional components for your JSF application?

198: How do you customize error pages?

199: How can a JSF application be tested?

200: What does Request Encoding do in JSF?

HR Questions

1: Tell me about yourself?
2: Why did you leave your last job?
3: What experience do you have in this field?
4: Do you consider yourself successful?
5: What do co-workers say about you?
6: What do you know about this organization?
7: What have you done to improve your knowledge in the last year?
8: Are you applying for other jobs?
9: Why do you want to work for this organization?
10: Do you know anyone who works for us?
11: What kind of salary do you need?
12: Are you a team player?
13: How long would you expect to work for us if hired?
14: Have you ever had to fire anyone? How did you feel about that?
15: What is your philosophy towards work?
16: If you had enough money to retire right now, would you?
17: Have you ever been asked to leave a position?
18: Explain how you would be an asset to this organization.
19: Why should we hire you?
20: Tell me about a suggestion you have made.
21: What irritates you about co-workers?
22: What is your greatest strength?
23: Tell me about your dream job or what are you looking for in a job?
24: Why do you think you would do well at this job?
25: What do you find the most attractive about this position? (Least attractive?)
26: What kind of person would you refuse to work with?
27: What is more important to you: the money or the work?
28: What would your previous supervisor say your strongest point is?
29: Tell me about a problem you had with a supervisor.
30: What has disappointed you about a job?
31: Tell me about your ability to work under pressure.
32: Do your skills match this job or another job more closely?
33: What motivates you to do your best on the job?
34: Are you willing to work overtime? Nights? Weekends?
35: How would you know you were successful on this job?
36: Would you be willing to relocate if required?
37: Are you willing to put the interests of the organization ahead of your own?
38: Describe your management style.
39: What have you learned from mistakes on the job?

40: Do you have any blind spots?
41: If you were hiring a person for this job, what would you look for?
42: Do you think you are overqualified for this position?
43: How do you propose to compensate for your lack of experience?
44: What qualities do you look for in a boss?
45: Tell me about a time when you helped resolve a dispute between others.
46: What position do you prefer on a team working on a project?
47: Describe your work ethic.
48: What has been your biggest professional disappointment?
49: Tell me about the most fun you have had on the job.
50: What would you do for us? (What can you do for us that someone else can't?)
51: Do you have any questions for me?

Some of the following titles might also be handy:

1. Oracle / PLSQL Interview Questions
2. ASP.NET Interview Questions
3. VB.NET Interview Questions
4. .NET Framework Interview Questions
5. C#.NET Interview Questions
6. OOPS Interview Questions
7. Core Java Interview Questions
8. JSP-Servlet Interview Questions
9. EJB (J2EE) Interview Questions
10. ADO.NET Interview Questions
11. SQL Server Interview Questions
12. C & C++ Interview Questions
13. 200 (HR) Interview Questions
14. JavaScript Interview Questions
15. JAVA/J2EE Interview Questions
16. Oracle DBA Interview Questions
17. XML Interview Questions
18. UNIX Shell Programming Interview Questions
19. PHP Interview Questions
20. J2ME Interview Questions
21. Hardware and Networking Interview Questions
22. Data Structures & Algorithms Interview Questions
23. Oracle E-Business Suite Interview Questions
24. UML Interview Questions
25. HTML, XHTML & CSS Interview Questions
26. JDBC Interview Questions
27. Hibernate, Springs & Struts Interview Questions
28. Linux Interview Questions

www.ingramcontent.com/pod-product-compliance
Lightning Source LLC
Chambersburg PA
CBHW052148070326
40689CB00050B/2517

9781461016687